SO-AIE-257

Library of Congress Cataloging-in-Publication Data

Fitzpatrick, Julie.
   Wheels/Julie Fitzpatrick: illustrated by Diana Bowles.
     p. cm.—(Science spirals)
   Includes index.
   Summary: Text, illustrations, and experiments demonstrate the
capabilities of wheels on vehicles, in pulleys and gears, and as
windmills and waterwheels.
   ISBN 0-382-09534-0
   1. Wheels—Juvenile literature. [1. Wheels—Experiments.
2. Experiments.] I. Bowles, Diana, ill. II. Title. III. Series.
TJ181.5.F573 1988
531.8—dc19   87-27592
                                                CIP
                                                AC

First published in Great Britain in 1986 by
Hamish Hamilton Children's Books
27 Wrights Lane, London W8 5SL

Adapted and first published in the United States in 1988 by
Silver Burdett Press Inc., Englewood Cliffs, New Jersey

Impreso por Edime, Org. Gráfica, S. A. (Mostoles) MADRID
I.S.B.N. 84-599-2491-2 Depósito legal M 32 355-1988
IMPRESO EN ESPAÑA PRINTED IN SPAIN

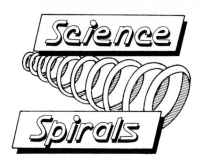

Wheels

Julie Fitzpatrick

Illustrated by Diana Bowles

Silver Burdett Press
Englewood Cliffs, New Jersey

Equipment you need for experiments in this book:

Let's Get Moving: *large book, containers of different shapes*

Rolling Along: *cylinders, heavy box, straight stick*

Making Wheels: *plastic lids, thread spools, cardboard circles, sticks, plastic straws, wire, pipe cleaners or knitting needles, nail, glue, putty, boxes*

Road Surfaces: *toy vehicle, stones, string, thin rubber band*

Slipping and Sliding: *toy vehicle, piece of plastic, tray of ice, cooking oil*

Tires: *shoes with ridged soles, shoes with smooth soles*

Ball Bearings: *marbles or round beads, shallow lid, can to fit inside lid*

Pulley Wheels: *stick, cardboard cylinder, string, modeling clay, shopping bag*

Winding It Up: *margarine tub, long nail, hammer, piece of wood, string, marbles*

Gear Wheels: *cardboard, corks, toothpicks*

Wheels with a Belt Drive: *thread spools, plastic lids, long nails, hammer, long rubber bands, piece of wood*

Moving Up and Down: *cardboard, paper fasteners, scissors*

Windmills: *corks, toothpicks, cardboard, tape*

Waterwheels: *scissors, rectangular plastic lid, adhesive putty, stick or pencil*

A Vehicle with Power: *4 wheels, 2 wooden axles, box for chassis, rubber band, string, toothpick*

Contents

Let's Get Moving

Which of these shapes move most
easily?
Find some objects shaped like these.

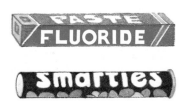

Get a large book to make a slope.
Put each shape at one end of the
book.
How high do you have to lift the slope to
make each shape move?
What is different about the way in which
the shapes move?

The cylinders roll.
The other shapes slide.
Cylinders move most easily.

Rolling Along

How can you move a heavy load?

Can you think of a way to use rolling cylinders to move a heavy load?

If you put cylinders under the load they will roll and move it along. Long ago, people used logs as rollers under a load.
What happens as your load passes over the rollers?

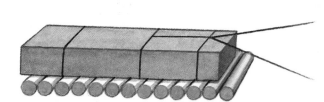

New rollers must be put in front each time.
Is there an easier way to move the load?

The rollers need a stick or rod to
turn on.
The rod can be fixed to the load.
Then the rollers keep carrying the
load along.

People found it easier to chop the logs
into pieces.
This may be how the wheel was first
made or invented.

The rod that a wheel turns on is
called an axle.
Some wheels looked like this.
How are they different from the
wheels we use?

Where have you seen wheels being used?

Wheels are used to make things move. They are used on vehicles.

Wheels are used in machinery.

Making Wheels

Here is one way to make a pair of wheels:

YOU NEED
straight stick
plastic lids
nail
putty

Must the axle be fixed to the center
of each wheel?
Try putting the axle in different places.
How do the wheels move?

The axle must be fixed to the center to
make the wheels run smoothly.

Here is a quick way to find the center of a circle.

Get some paper and trace around the wheel.

Cut out the circle. Fold it in half and then into quarters.

The center is where the fold lines cross.

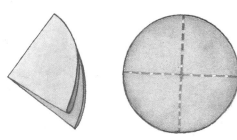

Put the paper circle over the wheel and mark the center.

Must the wheels on one axle be the same size?

Try using one large wheel and one small wheel.

How do the wheels move?

Why do wheels have to be round?

Here are some more ways to make
wheels:

YOU NEED

   *thread spools, circles of cardboard,
      yogurt lids (wheels)*
   *sticks, knitting needles, plastic
      straws, pipe cleaners or pieces of
      wire (axles)*
   a nail
   glue
   putty
   boxes

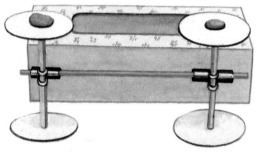

Test the wheels.
Do they run smoothly?
You could use putty to make
them stronger and keep them
from bending.
How could you improve, or make
the wheels better?
Look for other materials to use.

The frame of a vehicle is called the
chassis.
Build a chassis for your vehicle.

Steering Wheels

A steering wheel is used to make a
vehicle change direction.
The steering wheel is connected to
the front axle.
When the steering wheel is turned to
the right, the front wheels turn to the
right.
When the steering wheel is turned to
the left, the front wheels turn to
the left.

Design a model vehicle with a front
axle that can be turned to the right
and to the left.
What could be used to steer the
vehicle?

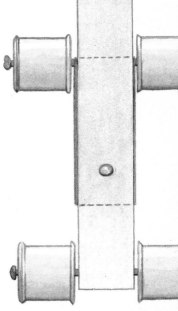

Road Surfaces

What happens if you move a vehicle
over rocky or muddy ground?
People began to use wheels for travel
but they needed better roads.
Which surface helps the wheels to run
smoothly? (The surface is the outside of
an object.)

Try moving a vehicle, or try roller
skating, over different surfaces.
Over which surfaces do the wheels roll
most easily?

You can measure how easily the vehicle moves over different surfaces. Use the stretch of a rubber band to show how the surface pushes against the vehicle.

YOU NEED
a toy vehicle loaded with stones
string
a thin rubber band

WHAT YOU DO
1. Tie one end of the string to the vehicle.
Tie the other end to the rubber band.

2. Pull the vehicle over different surfaces.

How far does the rubber band stretch each time?
Over which surfaces does the vehicle move easily?

Slipping and Sliding

A smooth surface is best for wheels but sometimes the surface can be slippery.
What can happen to a vehicle if there is ice on the road?

Vehicles can skid on icy roads. The wheels cannot grip the slippery surface.

What happens if there is oil on the road?
Pour some cooking oil down the middle of a plastic slope.
Let the vehicle roll down across the slope.
What happens to the vehicle when it runs into the oil?

Oil and ice come between the wheels and the road surface. The surfaces do not grip or rub together very well.

Oil on the road is dangerous but putting oil on bicycle parts is useful. The oil helps the parts to move more smoothly.

Tires

Tires are made of rubber.
They help the wheels grip the road.

Look at the pattern of ridges on a tire.
This pattern is called the tread.
Why do tires have a tread?

The ridges rub against the surface of
the road.
Rainwater on the tire can run away
between the ridges.

Some boots and shoes have ridges
on the soles.
Find one shoe with a ridged sole,
and one with a smooth sole.
Which one slides more easily?
The tread on an old pair of shoes
may be worn smooth in places.
The rubbing of the sole against
the ground wears down the tread.
This happens to tires.
Why is it dangerous to have tires
with a worn tread?

Putting on the Brakes

How do you stop the wheels from
turning when you are riding a bicycle?
You put on the brakes.
The brakes are pads of rubber.
When you use the brake handles the
pads press against the wheel.
This stops the wheel from turning.
The brake pads become worn down
by rubbing against the wheel.

Design a brake for a model vehicle.
Here is one idea.

Ball Bearings

In the wheels of some roller skates and skateboards you can see small silver colored balls.
These are called ball bearings.
Spin the wheels and see how smoothly they move.
Find out how ball bearings work.

YOU NEED

some marbles or round beads
lid just deep enough to hold the marbles
can to fit inside the lid

WHAT YOU DO

1. First put the can in the lid without the marbles.
How well does it turn?

2. Now put the marbles in the lid. Make the can turn on top of the marbles.
What difference do the marbles make?

Ball bearings are used in machines to help stop the parts from rubbing together.
Ball bearings help wheels to turn more easily.

Pulley Wheels

A pulley is a wheel with rope around it.
It is used to lift and lower heavy loads.
Make a pulley.

YOU NEED
  stick
  cardboard cylinder
  string
  modeling clay
  shopping bag to lift

WHAT YOU DO
1. Tie a long piece of string to the
handles of the bag.
Try lifting the bag up by the string.

2. Put the cylinder onto the stick.
Put the string over the cylinder.
Have a friend hold both ends of the
stick.
Now pull on the string to lift the bag.

Is it easier to pull up or to pull
down on the string?
A pulley makes it easier because
you use your weight to pull down.

Did the string slip off the cylinder?
Why do you think a pulley wheel
has a groove?
You could put clay on the ends of
the cylinder to make a groove
in the middle.

Winding It Up

You can fix rope to a load and
then use a wheel to wind it up.
Sailors once used a capstan wheel
to lift up the ship's anchor.
Make a model and see how
the wheel works.

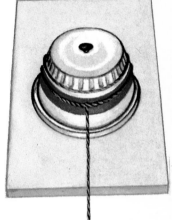

YOU NEED
   margarine or butter tub
   long nail
   hammer
   wood for the base
   string
   marbles or washers for weights

WHAT YOU DO
1. Hammer the nail into the wood.
Make a hole in the tub and put it over
the nail.
Test to see that the tub turns smoothly.

2. Cut a long piece of string.
Tie one end around the tub.
Tie the other end to a bag of marbles.

3. Turn the wheel to wind up the string.
What happens to the load?
What happens when you let the wheel
go?

4. How could you make this machine
easier to use?

Gear Wheels

In some machines, wheels are used to
turn other wheels.
These are called gear wheels.
Some gear wheels have teeth around
the outside, which are called cogs.
The cogs of one wheel fit, or mesh, into
the cogs of another.
The wheel that is moved first is called
the drive wheel.
The other wheels are called followers.

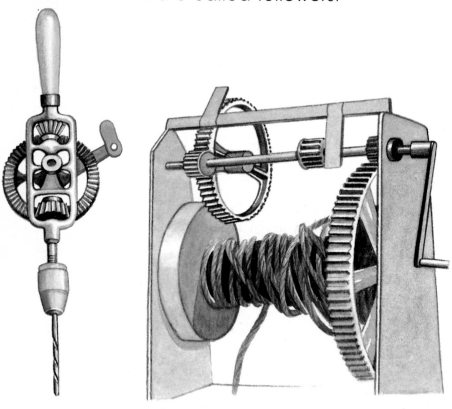

Make a model using gear wheels:

YOU NEED
> *cardboard from a cereal box*
> *two or three small corks*
> *toothpicks*

WHAT YOU DO

1. Break five toothpicks in half.
Push eight toothpicks into a cork to
make a star shape.
Push one toothpick into each end of
the cork to make the axle.
Do the same with another cork.

2. Hold one wheel in each hand.
Turn them to make the toothpicks
mesh together.
Which way do the wheels turn?

3. Use the cardboard to make a
stand for the wheels.
Fold the cardboard to make
a corner.
Put a wheel on each side of the fold
to make the wheels mesh together.
Find the best place for the wheels
and push the axles through the
cardboard.

4. You could decorate the corks to
make pinwheels.
Could you add another gear wheel?
Turn one wheel and watch the others
spin!

Wheels with a Belt Drive

Some machines have wheels
joined by a belt or a chain.
The belt is used to make the wheels
move. It is called a belt drive.

How to make a belt drive:

YOU NEED

thread spools and plastic lids
long nails
hammer
long rubber bands
piece of wood for the base

WHAT YOU DO

1. Hammer two nails into the wood,
about 4 inches apart.

2. Put spools over the nails. Stretch a
rubber band around both spools.

3. Turn the drive wheel.
How does the follower move?

4. Turn the drive wheel in the
other direction.
What happens to the follower?
How is this different from two
cog wheels working together?

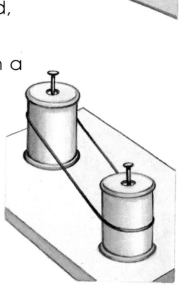

What happens if you use a
cross-over belt?
Make a belt drive using one large,
and one small spool. Mark each spool
with a spot drawn on it.
Turn the large spool once.
What happens to the smaller spool?
Turn the smaller spool once.
What happens to the large spool?

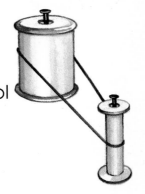

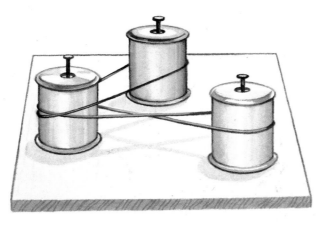

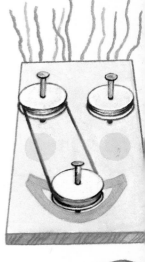

Make a toy with two spools for eyes
and one for a mouth.
How can you use rubber bands to
turn the mouth and
   a) make the eyes turn in the same
direction?
   b) make the eyes turn in opposite
directions?

Moving Up and Down

Wheels can be used to make objects move up and down. Make a model to see how they work.

YOU NEED
> cardboard from an empty
>   cereal box
> paper fasteners
> scissors

WHAT YOU DO

1. Cut out a wheel shaped like this.

2. Use a paper fastener to fix it to a larger piece of cardboard.

3. Cut a long strip of cardboard. Use another paper fastener to fix it to the wheel.

4. Turn the wheel and watch how the strip of cardboard moves.
It goes up and down.
As the wheel turns, it pushes objects up and down.

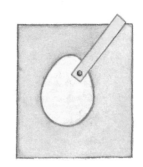

Make a toy that moves up and
down as a wheel turns.
Use cardboard and paper
fasteners.

How could you make a haunted house
with ghosts that move up and down?

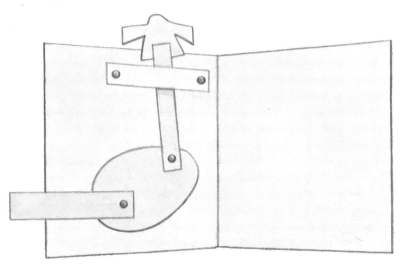

Windmills

Wheels are used in windmills.
They turn the machinery for
grinding grain.
The wind makes the sails turn.
This makes the wheels turn
inside the windmill.
Try making a windmill.

YOU NEED
> *a cork or a piece of styrofoam*
> *toothpicks*
> *cardboard*
> *tape*
> *scissors*

WHAT YOU DO
1. Make the sails of the windmill
like this.

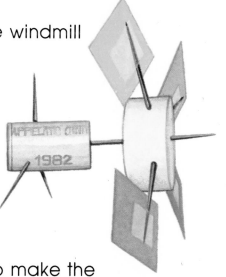

2. Blow onto the sails to make the
windmill turn.

Waterwheels

A waterwheel is turned by water
running around it.
The waterwheel is used to turn
machinery.
Can you make a waterwheel?

YOU NEED
> *rectangular plastic lid*
> *blob of adhesive putty*
> *stick or a pencil*
> *scissors*

WHAT YOU DO
1. Cut the plastic lid to make
the blades of the waterwheel.

2. Roll the putty into a ball.
Thread the pencil through the
center of the putty.

3. Press the blades into the putty.

4. Turn on the water.
Hold the waterwheel under
the running water.
Try running the water slowly and
then quickly.
What happens to the waterwheel?

A Vehicle with Power

Make a vehicle that moves by using the power in a rubber band.

YOU NEED

four wheels
two wooden axles
a box for the chassis
rubber band
string
toothpick

WHAT YOU DO

1. Make the vehicle.
Fix the wheels to the axle.
Test to see that the axle turns smoothly.

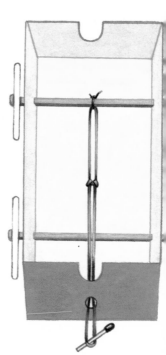

2. Make a hole at the front of the chassis.
Thread a rubber band through the hole.
Keep it in place with the toothpick.

3. Use the string to tie the other end of the rubber band to the back axle.
Turn the back wheels to wind the rubber band around the back axle.
What happens as you let the wheels go?

4. How could you use the rubber band to make the vehicle go backwards?